KING EDGAR

by

HELEN PANTER

MORGAN BOOKS

37 BROAD STREET, BATH, ENGLAND

First published in 1971
© Helen Panter

903044 03 X

Made and Printed in Great Britain by
COWARD & GERRISH LTD., LARKHALL, BATH, SOMERSET

Preface

This compilation from Medieval, Victorian, and Modern sources, is an attempt to look at the personality and the achievements of King Edgar, who was crowned in Bath a thousand years ago, against the background of his times. It is intended for those who have only a slight knowledge of the Anglo-Saxon period, and of Edgar's place among the great Kings of Wessex.

Up to the present only one scholar of repute has attempted any detailed study of King Edgar and his contemporaries. Most of our information comes from the near contemporary lives of the great prelates with whom he worked so closely, and from less reliable medieval sources.

A great deal of research on the Anglo-Saxon period has been going on over the last century, but a modern, detailed, and scholarly, study of this great king has yet to come. The distinguished nineteenth-century scholar E. W. Robertson added an interesting study of Edgar and his contemporaries to his *Historical Essays* published in 1872.

Robertson was possibly attracted to Edgar because he had, in his opinion, been harshly judged by posterity. To use his own words, Edgar's annals had been written "without regard to historic evidence or decent loyalty". Strictly speaking, this idea would not be acceptable today. Edgar has had his full share of adulation. If he has had more than his fair share of slander, no great harm has been done. Most historians today ignore altogether the irresponsible and unreliable ballad stories that have come down to us mostly from post-conquest writers. Some may accept the possibility of one or two youthful indiscretions, but all would agree that Edgar was a sincerely religious man, and the last truly great king of the Royal House of Wessex.

The questions most likely to be asked about King Edgar's Bath coronation of 973 are: "Why was Edgar not crowned until he had reigned as undisputed king of England for fourteen years?" "Why should he choose to be crowned in Bath instead of Kingston-on-Thames where other tenth-century kings of England appear to have been crowned and anointed?"

This brief study of King Edgar's reign and his coronation in Bath should supply the answers to these questions, but since we are looking back to events which happened a thousand years ago, some lack of evidence is inevitable.

Acknowledgements

I am grateful to Professor D. Whitelock for reading and commenting on my work in manuscript, and for introducing me to Dr. Janet L. Nelson of King's College, London, who generously allowed me to use some of the results of her, as yet, unpublished research on 'King-Making' and 'The Coronation Order of the Tenth Century'. As a result of the information given to me by Dr. Nelson I rewrote the section on the Coronation Order which had formerly been based almost wholly on the classic work on that subject, *The History of the English Coronation* by P. E. Schramm. I retained a good deal of this work, but I am indebted to Dr. Nelson for more up-to-date information.

I am also grateful to Dr. E. A. Fisher for his careful reading of the final draft, and to my husband who was also my very patient typist.

Finally, I acknowledge with gratitude the very wide-ranging facilities made available to me through the City of Bath Reference and Lending Libraries. Any errors that remain are my own.

HELEN PANTER

Contents

THE ROYAL HOUSE OF WESSEX
(The House of Egbert)

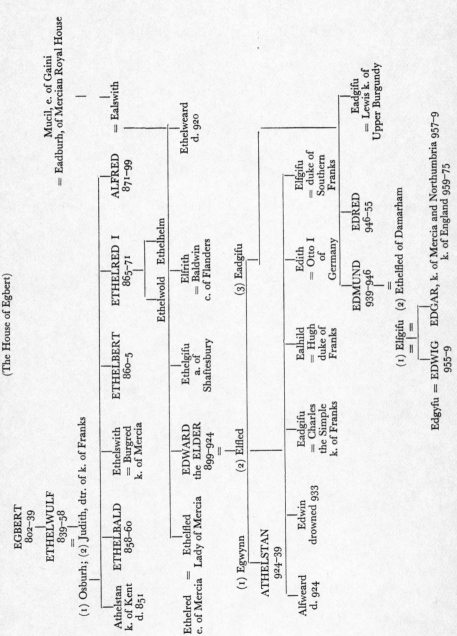

a. abbess; c. count; d. died; e. ealdorman; k. king.

Introduction

A thousand years ago, in the year 973, a magnificent ceremony took place in Bath. Edgar, son of Edmund of the Royal House of Wessex, was anointed and crowned King of all England.

The *Anglo-Saxon Chronicle* recorded the event with twelve lines of verse. The following is an extract:

" ... 973 In this year Edgar, ruler of the English, with a great company was consecrated king in the ancient borough, Acemannesceaster—the men who dwell in this island also call it by another name—Bath.

"There, great joy had come to all on that blessed day which the children of men call and name the day of Pentecost.

"There, was assembled a crowd of priests, a great throng of learned monks, as I have heard tell. . . .

"And Edmund's son, bold in battle, had spent twenty nine years in the world when this came about, and then in the thirtieth was consecrated king."

With those twelve lines of verse the chronicler marked the Bath coronation as an event of outstanding importance, and Edgar's solemn anointing in 973 was indeed different from any earlier English coronation.

In the first place, it was not Edgar's inauguration to kingship. This ceremony occurred sixteen years earlier in 957 when, at the age of fourteen he became king of England north of the river Thames. After his brother Edwig's death in 959 he had ruled as undisputed king of all England for 14 years.

Edgar was not the first of his house to merit this title. Alfred's eldest grandson and Edgar's uncle, Athelstan throughout the last twelve years of his reign was not only the sole ruler of England and acknowledged overlord of most of Britain, he also exerted more influence on continental affairs than Edgar or any member of the Royal House of Wessex.

Athelstan's successors, Edmund and Edred, were consecrated as kings of England but spent much time during their reigns in driving out Norse kings who had managed to establish their rule over Northumbria. Edgar's brother, Edwig, was consecrated king of England in 955, but the party surrounding the fifteen-year-old king was not acceptable outside Wessex, and all England north of the Thames elected the younger brother Edgar as king in 957, thereby avoiding the possibility of internal strife.

The joyful ceremony at Bath was held only two years before the end of Edgar's memorable reign. There was indeed good cause for celebration in the year 973, for under Edgar's firm rule and for the first time in its history, the English nation had been united in peace and prosperity, in a land free from all foreign invaders and from internal strife. It was for this reason that this great king in after years was referred to as 'Edgar the Peaceful'.

At the Bath coronation the king received the anointing as of a bishop of the English Church. Edgar's was the first anointing of an English king to be described and documented. It was a precedent, and a pattern upon which future coronations were based. It was possibly the final 'take over' by the English Church of the king-making ceremony, raising the status of English kingship, setting the king apart from other men, as the anointed of God, the patron and protector of the English church and nation and lord (emperor) of Britain.

A nineteenth-century historian describes the coronation at Bath as:

"A solemn typical enunciation of English unity. An inauguration of the king of all the nations of England, celebrated by two archbishops, possibly with special instructions from Rome, possibly in imitation of the imperial consecration of Edgar's kinsmen, the first and second Ottos (as German Emperors), possibly as a declaration of the imperial character of the English crown itself."[1]

Perhaps this ceremony could be more simply described as a 'status symbol'.

As Robertson suggests in the above quotation, continental custom may have influenced Edgar in his decision to be anointed in the year 973, although we are told that he was already crowned, presumably consecrated, and a firmly established, undisputed ruler.

There was no lack of communication with the continent in Edgar's time. The great prelates and reformers of the English church were in close touch with continental ecclesiastics. Edgar himself was related by marriage to half a dozen continental rulers. His uncle, Otto the first, Saxon ruler of the united East Frankish provinces (Germany) had, in 962, been created Holy Roman Emperor by Pope John XII. Otto the second, the younger son of the emperor was also anointed as Holy Roman Emperor in the year 967 and succeeded his father who died in 973.

From the eighth century onwards it had become the custom for Frankish kings to be anointed and crowned by the Pope as patrons and protectors of the church in Western Europe. The heir, or heirs, were usually crowned during the father's lifetime in order to secure the succession. The German emperor continued this custom.

In England, the patron and protector of the church was Edgar of the Royal House of Wessex. It may just be a coincidence that, in 973, when his friend and ally Otto the second became sole emperor of the four united German provinces, that Edgar was anointed as king of the three united English provinces, Wessex, Mercia and Northumbria, and lord of all Britain.

Another reason why the year 973 was chosen for the anointing has been suggested by Sir Frank Stenton who says:

" (Archbishop) Dunstan, like many Frankish churchmen of his age, was strongly influenced by the parallel between the anoining of a king and the consecration of a priest. . . .

"It is probably something more than mere coincidence that the year of his coronation was the year in which he reached the age of thirty, below which no one could canonically be ordained to the priesthood."[2]

From the ninth century onwards, ecclesiastical consecration came to play an increasingly important role in legitimising royal power in the various kingdoms of Western Europe: by the tenth century anointing had become essential.

LOTHIAN

STRATHCLYDE

NORTHUMBRIA

Jarrow

York

Lincoln

Offa's Dyke

Dore

Nottingham

Derby

Lichfield

Stamford

Leicester

Tamworth

Peterborough

MERCIA

Ramsey

Ely

WALES

Worcester

Hereford

Oxford

Abingdon

Gloucester

London

Malmesbury

Bath

Chippenham

Kingston

Cheddar

Frome

Canterbury

WESSEX

Glastonbury

Winchester

TENTH CENTURY
ENGLAND

CHAPTER ONE

The Unification of England

The political unification of Anglo-Saxon England was a gradual process which had been going on since the settlement of the Angles and Saxons in this island in the sixth century. At the beginning of the seventh century there were eleven or twelve separate small Anglo-Saxon kingdoms each with its own king. When these kingdoms were not at war with the Britons or the Welsh, as they were called later, they were at war with each other. First one kingdom and then another would gain ascendency, and its ruler would claim supremacy over his neighbours. A supremacy south of the Thames, south of the Humber, or north of the Humber, was usually meant, not over the whole of England.

Gradually the smaller and weaker kingdoms were absorbed by those more powerful, until the number was reduced to seven in the eighth century and in the ninth century to three large kingdoms: Northumbria, Mercia, and Wessex. The names of some of those small seventh- and eighth-century kingdoms survive today as county or district names, notably, Kent, Sussex, East Anglia, and Wessex.

Bede, the great eighth-century historian, described these overlords as Bretwaldas, or Britain rulers, and listed them, omitting the great Mercian overlord who was just before his time. The *Anglo-Saxon* chronicler copied this list, still omitting the great Mercian overlords, although they had been the most powerful:

1) Aelle—king of the South Saxons . . late fifth century
2) Ceawlin—king of the West Saxons . . sixth century
3) Ethelbert of Kent . . . . late sixth century
4) Redwald—king of the East Angles . . seventh century
5) Edwin—king of Northumbria . . early seventh century
6) Oswald—king of Northumbria . . early seventh century

7) Oswy—king of Northumbria   .   .   . seventh century

Omitted { 1. Wulfhere of Mercia   .   . late seventh century
         2. Ethelbald of Mercia   .   .   . eighth century
         3. Offa of Mercia   .   .   . late eighth century

8) Egbert—king of the West Saxons .   . early ninth century

Stenton suggests that Bretwalda was little more than an honorific title accorded to the strongest ruler of his time.

From this list it will be seen that the overlordship passed from one kingdom to another until it finally came to Egbert of Wessex, the grandfather of Alfred the Great. It is from the House of Egbert that our monarchy can claim descent, and Egbert traced his ancestry back to Cerdic the early sixth-century leader of the West Saxons.

The most powerful of the overlords were the great Mercian kings of the eighth century. King Ethelbald ruled southern England for almost thirty years. His was a military rule, and he was eventually murdered by his own bodyguard. His successor, King Offa, also achieved supremacy by strife and bloodshed, but he held it by statesmanship and the power of his personality. It is generally agreed that he, more than any other ruler, prepared the way for Alfred and his descendants to unite England under Wessex rule, after they had so valiantly released the country from the Danish and Norse warlords.

In the eighth century Offa had signed his charters 'Rex Anglorum'— King of the English, and 'Rex totius Anglorum patriae'—King of the whole land of the English. He ruled England outside his own Mercia as overlord, but he was regarded by Charlemagne, with whom he negotiated on terms of equality, as king of England, and he was the first English king to play an independent part in continental affairs.

The supremacy of Alfred was of a different kind. All the people outside the Danish province of the East Midlands, East Anglia and Northumbria south of the Tyne submitted to him in 886 as their protector and leader. The Mercians submitted to his son Edward the Elder who, with the help of his famous sister 'The Lady of Mercia', recovered the East Midlands and East Anglia from the Danish warlords.

The Viking invasions, Danish and Norse, themselves played no small part in uniting the country under the leadership of the kings of Wessex. Alfred's grandsons Athelstan, Edmund and Edred finally completed the unification of England. Their determined opposition to the Norse Vikings freed the country from these foreign invaders and all the nations of England submitted to them. They were the first members of the Royal House of Wessex to use the title 'King of All England'.

CHAPTER TWO

Edgar and his Family

Edgar was born in 943 or 944, it is not known where. He never knew either of his parents for his mother, Elfgifu, died soon after his birth—she was buried in Shaftesbury Abbey—and his father, King Edmund, was stabbed to death at Pucklechurch in Gloucestershire about three years later, and was buried in Glastonbury Abbey.

King Edmund had succeeded his half-brother King Athelstan in 939 at the age of eighteen, and was soon engaged in fighting Norse invaders of the Midlands and the North. His campaigns were ultimately successful and in 942 he expelled the Norsemen from the East Midlands to the great delight of the Danish population, by this time loyal subjects of the king of England.

At Cheddar in Somerset there was a royal palace where Edmund spent much of his time. It was while he was hunting at Cheddar that he nearly lost his life in an incident that had an important sequel. The king's companions had become separated from him as he chased a stag through the woods to the top of the gorge. The terrified stag and the hounds at its heels rushed madly over the edge of the cliff. The king's horse galloping out of control close behind, looked likely to follow them. Realising the danger, the king did what many other men have done when death seemed imminent, he prayed. At that time there was a monk connected with the royal court with whom the king had quarrelled. His name was Dunstan and he was distantly related to the royal family. During those few moments when the king clung to his horse and prayed, the thought that he had wronged Dunstan flashed through his mind. He vowed that if his life was spared he would make amends. The horse did stop in time at the edge of the cliff and Edmund escaped without injury. The king kept his vow, made his peace with Dunstan, and installed him as Abbot of Glastonbury Abbey. Dunstan, who had been educated at Glastonbury, spent many years as abbot of his beloved monastery where he established a rule of life for his monks;

acted as adviser to King Edmund and his successor; spent more than a year in exile; was recalled by Edgar to become bishop of Worcester and London, and, after 959, when Edgar became king of England, Dunstan succeeded to the see of Canterbury, which he held for 27 years. He was an outstanding statesman, a great archbishop and a moderate but able leader in the Monastic Revival and Reformation of the tenth century.

There was an unusual incident, connected with Bath, during Edmund's reign. In the year 944 the monks of St. Bertin's monastery at St. Omer in Flanders so strongly resisted the new rule of the great monastic reformer Gerard of Brogne that they were forced to leave their monastery. They fled to England where they were kindly received by King Edmund in gratitude for the burial they had given his half-brother Edwin, who had been drowned off the coast of Flanders in 933. The atheling (prince) Edwin must have been involved in some revolt against King Athelstan, his half-brother, about which nothing is known. He was evidently seeking refuge in Flanders when the shipwreck occurred. King Edmund remembered the kindness of the Flemish monks during this time of trouble and allowed them to settle in the monastery of Bath.[3] That any of these monks survived to witness Edgar's coronation in Bath nearly thirty years later is unlikely.

Edmund's tragic death occurred when he was still only twenty-four. It happened at Pucklechurch, about nine miles north of Bath, where he was dining with his court. The king's steward was attacked by a criminal newly returned from banishment: the king went to his man's aid and received fatal stab wounds. The *Anglo-Saxon* chronicler describes Edmund as:

" . . . lord of the English, protector of men, the beloved performer of mightier deeds, defender of warriors."

Edmund, like his great grandson and namesake Edmund Ironside, was a potentially great king of Wessex who died on the threshold of greatness.

Edmund left two infant sons, Edwig aged about six, and Edgar who was three. He was succeeded by his brother Edred, a young man of about twenty-two years who was consecrated, and crowned king of England by Oda, the archbishop of Canterbury in the year 946.

King Edred's health was not good, he suffered from a gastric disorder which must have given him years of pain and eventually caused his death at an early age. He was supported by his mother, queen Edgifu, and by Dunstan abbot of Glastonbury, his closest friend and adviser. Less than two years after his accession Edred led a successful campaign against the Viking king Eric Bloodaxe who had sailed from Norway and established himself as king in York. Eric was very soon succeeded in Northumbria by an Irish-Norse leader Olaf, who held that Kingdom for three years, only to be driven out by the return of Eric Bloodaxe in 952. Eric reigned in York until 954 in which year he was finally driven out by the Northumbrians and slain. Northumbria once again submitted to the king of England.

King Edred after a long illness, died the following year, 955, at the royal palace of Frome in Somerset.

Edwig, the elder of Edmund's two young sons succeeded his uncle Edred. A weakly boy of fifteen he succeeded to a kingdom now free of Norse invaders, and was consecrated and crowned king of England presumably at Kingston-on-Thames where Anglo-Saxon kings of England since Athelstan's time seem to have been consecrated.

The boy king, who was known by the nickname of 'eall faeger'— all fair—because of his beauty of face and person, and who was described by his kinsman Ethelweard as 'well beloved,' was much under the influence of a lady of high rank named Ethelgifu, who was thought by later authorities to have been his foster mother. He was also deeply attached to her young daughter Elfgifu, who may have been his distant cousin.

After his coronation, and the great banquet that followed, a celebration which probably went on for many hours and which must have been an exhausting experience for one so young, Edwig escaped from the gathering of ealdormen and bishops and sought relaxation in the company of the ladies Ethelgifu and Elfgifu. When his absence had been noticed and deplored, Dunstan and the bishop of Lichfield were asked to recall him to his kingly duties. There was a most undignified scene. Edwig was so reluctant to leave the two ladies and return to the assembly that the two churchmen were obliged to use force. The lady Elfgifu was considered to be an unsuitable companion for the young king being too closely related to him, either as foster sister or distant cousin.

Some time after this event Edwig and Elfgifu were married having disregarded all opposition, and the disapproval of the king's spiritual advisers. Dunstan who had incurred the emnity of the new queen's mother and her party, now in power, was soon obliged to leave the country. He went to Ghent where he found a welcome at the monastery of Blandinium. The king's grandmother, the old queen-mother Edgifu was also obliged to leave the court, and was deprived of her lands and status.

Edgar, however, remained at his brother's court. The grants of land by Edwig to the monastery of Bath and other churches drawn up in 957 all bear Edgar's signature as testator.

According to the *Anglo-Saxon Chronicle* archbishop Oda separated Edwig and Elfgifu "because they were too closely related". Whether this actually happened is very doubtful, as Queen Elfgifu, wife of King Edwig, is mentioned in the *Liber Vitae* of Winchester as an illustrious benefactor.

It is hoped that the unfortunate Edwig was not separated from his young wife as he died in 959 at the age of nineteen.

The party surrounding the young king Edwig and his mother-in-law the lady Ethelgifu was unpopular outside Wessex, and in 957 Merica and Northumbria revolted. There was no military action, but the kingdom was divided. Edwig remained as king in Wessex and ruled the country south of the Thames, and his brother Edgar at the age of fourteen, succeeded as king of Mercia and Northumbria, that is, all England north of the Thames. This division of the kingdom appears to have been the outcome of power politics in which the royal brothers were too young to have taken any part.

The whole country was reunited under one king when Edwig died in 959, and Edgar added his native Wessex to his kingdom as his brother's heir and chosen successor.

Edgar the King

Edgar the Peaceful is an unusual title for a ruler who maintained internal peace, and kept England free from foreign invaders by a great display of naval and military strength.

A near contemporary writer says of Edgar:

"He put his feet on his enemies' necks, so that not only the rulers of the islands feared him greatly, but also the kings of several peoples, learning of his 'prudentia' were struck with fear and terror."[4]

In the late tenth century there were Norse settlements on the Isle of Man, the Hebrides, and other islands off the north west coast of

Britain. It is to the rulers of these islands, no less than the princes of Wales and Scotland that the writer refers. All acknowledged the English king as their lord, placed themselves under his protection, and were prepared to go to his aid in the event of war.

When Edgar reached maturity he was obviously a powerful and forceful ruler, he was at the same time a man of sincere religious convictions. He has been described as not above average height and slightly built, but he was apparently a strong, athletic king and could give a good account of himself in any combat.

In the early years of his reign, for he ruled all England at the age of sixteen, Edgar was fortunate in having a most efficient and reliable group of ealdormen, most of whom could claim some degree of kinship with the king either by blood or marriage. Each of these ealdormen ruled his own province as the king's representative, and was responsible for military organisation and for the maintenance of law and order. In this way Edgar delegated his authority and government, and could draw on great military forces should the need arise. The *Chronicle* mentions only one occasion when "King Edgar ordered all Thanet (off the Kent coast) to be ravaged". The king's order for the military attack on Thanet in 969 was a result of brutal treatment of York merchants, visiting the island for the purpose of trade, by the inhabitants. There were, no doubt other occasions when the army was called upon to maintain law and order.

Edgar seems to have placed great reliance on the upkeep of an efficient naval force. It was a force to be reckoned with and Edgar appears to have taken a personal interest in it.

Every year, as soon as weather allowed, after Easter, he ordered his ships to be assembled on each coast. According to later sources there were three fleets, and Edgar sailed with each in turn. First with the eastern fleet towards the west. Then with the western fleet towards the north, and then with the northern fleet, presumably around Scotland to the east again, "carefully vigilant lest pirates should disturb the country".[5]

The king needed to be physically fit in Anglo-Saxon England!

Almost a century earlier, in 877, Alfred, the king's great grandfather, realising the necessity for a strong sea defence against the Danes, had commanded "that long ships should be built throughout the kingdom in order to offer battle as enemy approached".[6] There is a description in the *Chronicle* of the ships built for Alfred:

"They were almost twice as long as the others. Some had sixty oars, some more. They were built neither on Frisian (Netherlands) nor Danish pattern, but as it seemed to him (Alfred) that they could be most useful."

King Alfred fought several sea battles with the Danes, and his grandson King Athelstan, in 939, actually sent an English fleet to the aid of his young nephew, Louis of France, "the first occasion on which an English king is known to have assembled a fleet in order to help a continental ally".[7]

That Edgar's ships were probably built on a pattern similar to that of his great grandfather is shown in ecclesiastical records of his, and later, reigns. The bishops were not exempt from naval or military obligations, and more than one bishop seems to have been responsible for providing a shipful, 60 oarsmen, from his estate. The provision of a ship, too, appears in some diocesan records and charters.

We are told that at other times in the year (presumably when the weather allowed) the king travelled through the provinces and "made enquiry into the decisions of men in power, severely avenging violated laws."

The Anglo-Saxon code of law would seem to us harsh, but so would those of our Victorian ancestors. Some of Edgar's codes have come down to us, and a characteristic of these laws is his recognition that the Danes of the eastern provinces and Northumbria, were his loyal subjects, as they had been of his immediate predecessors. He allowed them to decide, with few exceptions, on the laws which best suited their own way of life:

"I have ever allowed them this, and I will allow it as long as my life lasts, because of your loyalty which you have always shown me".[8]

The king appointed bishops and ealdormen to rule over his Danish subjects but left them free to administer the laws as they chose.

It may be that Edgar's laws were not so very harsh as later writers imply, because we are told, that an oath to observe 'Edgar's Law' was taken by all members at a national assembly held in Oxford in 1017, at the beginning of Canute's reign.

Whatever Edgar owed to his ealdormen and the great churchmen during the early years of his reign, it is obvious that his own character, his statesmanship, energy, and ability, in the years of his maturity earned for him the respect and admiration of the nation.

The most distinguished Anglo-Saxon historian of this century comparing Edgar with the great kings who had preceded him, says:

"Modern historians, realising the significance of the ideals to which he gave his patronage, have tended to include him among the greatest of old English rulers. In part their praise is justified. It was a notable achievement to keep England secure against foreign enemies for sixteen years, and to maintain a standard of internal order which set a pattern for later generations. But when Edgar is compared with other outstanding members of his house—with Alfred or with Athelstan—he falls at once into a lower class than theirs. He was never required to defend English civilisation against barbarians from overseas, nor to deal with the problems raised by the existence of barbarian states within England itself. His part in history was to maintain the peace established in England by earlier kings. It is his distinction that he gave unreserved support to the men who were creating the environment of a new English culture by the reformation of English monastic life".[9]

Edgar and Scotland

Throughout the ninth century the Wessex kings had fought and finally subdued Danish invaders who in Alfred's time almost overran the whole of England. It was with an army of men from Wiltshire, Somerset, and Hampshire, that Alfred stemmed the tide of invasion by the decisive victory he gained at the battle of Edington in Wiltshire. Gradually the Danes were subdued and contained within boundaries agreed by Alfred, and his son Edward the Elder who, before his death in 924, had regained the whole of England south of the Humber, not without the help of his sister 'The Lady of Mercia.'

The tenth-century kings were threatened by a new army of invasion. The Norsemen from Scandinavia were overrunning Northumbria and parts of Mercia and the Danish East Midlands a few years before Edgar was born. Edgar's father and his two uncles, Athelstan, and Edred had all fought the Norse Vikings but Edgar, and his brother before him, succeeded to an England free of foreign invaders.

The Viking threat remained during Edgar's reign. All along the continental coast opposite the eastern shores of Britain there were Norse settlements, and along the east coast of Ireland. Edmund,

Edgar's father, had sought the allegiance of Malcom, king of the Scots against these invaders, by offering him the kingdom of Strathclyde, an area thought to have been bounded by the Solway Firth in the north, the rivers Eamont (near Penrith) and Derwent, to the south, and the Lake District mountains to the east. Strathclyde, once part of Northumbria, had a British, or Welsh king in the tenth century. It was a trouble spot, mainly inhabited by Britons and Irish-Norse immigrants. Malcolm soon lost it to its former British king.

Edgar was more successful in his dealings with the northern kings, who paid him homage after his Bath coronation. A significant incident was Edgar's meeting with Kenneth, king of the Scots. Kenneth paid homage to Edgar, who granted to him land on the eastern side of the country, between the rivers Tweed and Forth, then known as Lothian.

The terms of Edgar's grant are of interest, he ceded Lothian to Kenneth:

"On this condition, that every year at the principal festivals where the king and his successors wear their crowns, they, the kings of the Scots, should come to court and joyfully celebrate the feast with the rest of the nobles of the kingdom. Moreover the king gave him many residences on the way, so that he and his successors coming to the festivals and returning thence could be lodged there. And these remained in the possession of the kings of the Scots, until the time of Henry II".[10]

This agreement that Kenneth should attend court on the principal feast days, Christmas, Easter, and Whitsuntide, is accepted as evidence that 'crown wearings' were customary at these times in tenth-century England. No other evidence exists.

CHAPTER THREE

The Marriage Customs of the Anglo-Saxons

It is surprising that little or no information about the marriage customs of the Angles and Saxons after their settlement in this country has come down to us. They were of Germanic or Teutonic origin, and they came to England from what is now southern Denmark, and north west Germany. It was only by studying the marriage customs of the whole of north west Europe and of this country in later centuries, that Robertson was able to make comparisons, and to describe the marriage customs that the Anglo-Saxons probably brought with them to this country.

Looking back to the Anglo-Saxon period he makes two general observations: Marriage was not yet a sacrament of the church, divorce was easier and illegitimacy did not have the significance that we give it today. On the other hand the marriage customs he describes bear a remarkable similarity to those of today.

The Roman historian Tacitus, writing at the end of the first century A.D. (in his *Germania* 18–19) about the marriage customs of the Teutonic tribes from whom the Anglo-Saxons derive, says:

" . . . marriage in Germany is austere, and there is no feature in their morality that deserves higher praise . . . It is still better in those states in which only virgins marry, and the hopes and prayers of a wife are settled once and for all . . ."
"Good morality is more effective in Germany than good laws in some places that we know".

Edgar lived nearly nine centuries after Tacitus wrote, but a millenium separates this generation from Edgar's, and yet many of the traditions of his times still exist, modified perhaps, to suit the times.

The German tribes were pagan when Tacitus wrote. The Anglo-Saxons were pagan when they brought their marriage customs with them to this country.

In Northern Europe, as in England in the tenth century, there were two stages of matrimony. In other words, a marriage was begun and completed on two distinct and separate occasions.

The wedding was the first phase of the marriage, when the bride price was paid, and the terms were agreed on. This was a civil contract when 'weds', pledges or securities, were exchanged. Today the first phase of marriage is the engagement or betrothal period, and as we look upon an engagement as a probationary or preparatory period and not an irrevocable commitment, so the wedding of the Anglo-Saxons was looked upon as a probationary period and the marriage was finally completed at the Giving Away ceremony.

There is no certainty about the length of time which might elapse between the Anglo-Saxon wedding ceremony and the second stage of the marriage, the Giving Away ceremony, but the possibility of a child being born after the wedding and before the completion of the marriage suggests that it may have been as long as a year. A priest was present when the marriage was completed, to sanctify the legal union by his blessing, and the woman took on the marriage veil.

If a man or woman married for a second time, the priest was forbidden to bless the union, but the marriage was none the less legal and the offspring legitimate. According to Robertson, a child born during the first phase of a marriage, which was not then completed because one of the parties wished to withdraw, was a legitimate offspring. For either party to withdraw after the wedding ceremony was not an easy matter. The wedding was a marriage in the legal sense, and the inconstant partner (who wished to withdraw) not only forfeited all claim to the dowry and any other gifts which may have passed between the two, but was also expected to take over the responsibility for any child resulting from the union. The church also regarded the wedding as a binding contract, but seems to have accepted the possibility of withdrawal.

To a woman the dowry was essential, because the child of an undowered woman who had not been Given Away was illegitimate[11].

In later centuries, an uncompleted marriage, where the bride had not yet been Given Away, was known as a 'handfast' marriage. Marriage customs slowly changed over the centuries, and in the fifteenth century a previous handfast union was apparently a ground for divorce or annulment. Richard III's claim to the throne was based on the supposed illegitimacy of his brother's children, owing to Edward IV's 'betrothal' to another lady before his marriage with Elizabeth Woodville.

Thus briefly, we have Robertson's ideas on the marriage customs of Western Europe and Anglo-Saxon England in the tenth century. The continental sources he used are too remote and inaccessible to be mentioned here, but his opinions are too interesting to be omitted. It is essential to quote a reliable twentieth-century description for comparison:

"There were two parts to a marriage: the 'wedding' that is, the pledging or betrothal, when the bride-price was paid and the terms were agreed on; and the 'gift' the bridal itself, when the bride was given to the bridegroom, with feasting and ceremony. Ecclesiastical blessing was not necessary to the legality of the marriage, though the Church advocated it. The Church discouraged second marriages and advised priests to withhold their blessings from these."[12]

Edgar's Marriages

Much has been said, and written, and sung, about Edgar's marriages, but so little is known about the first two short and probably unhappy unions that much that has been written about them is now regarded as fiction.

Edgar must have married his first wife, a very beautiful young girl named Ethelfleda when he was barely eighteen years of age, and Edward his eldest son and heir was born of this union. What happened to Ethelfleda is not known. A very probable ending to this union was that Ethelfleda died in giving birth to her son. Another point of view is, that Edgar was persuaded to withdraw before the marriage was finally completed because Ethelfleda was not a lady of the highest rank and was not therefore a suitable consort for the king of England. This is borne out by the fact that Edgar, about the time of his marriage, raised her father Ordmaer to the rank of ealdorman. There is no real evidence that Edgar withdrew from the union, but it is certain that Edward, the child of the marriage, was brought up in his father's court as the legitimate heir.

Very soon after his marriage with Ethelfleda, perhaps within eighteen months, Edgar became deeply attached to a young girl named Wulfthrith. Even less is known about this union. A daughter was born, but Wulfthrith retired with her child to the nunnery at

Wilton. It is not known whether Wulfthrith became a nun, she would probably have been too young to take her final vows at the time of her daughter's birth or for some years after. Women did not take vows before the age of twenty-five, and many women of rank lived in nunneries without ever doing so. Wulfthrith's daughter Edith, who grew up and eventually became abbess of Wilton, died in her twenty-third year so she could not have taken vows either. Lay abbesses were not at all unusual in Anglo-Saxon England.

Robertson who has drawn his explanation of Edgar's union with Wulfthrith from an eleventh-century writer named Gotselin who wrote *The Life of St. Edith* (Wulfthrith's daughter) says that this affair with Wulfthrith has every appearance of a wedding in which the bride decided against the final ceremony of being Given Away to her husband, who, it is thought, wished to complete the marriage. She was thus the inconstant partner, and it was she who accepted the responsibilities of parenthood. In those times apparently she was able to do this without any stain on her character. How much reliance can be placed on this explanation is a matter for conjecture.

Edgar and his brother, burdened with the status, if not the full responsibilities of kingship at a very early age, must have been in a vulnerable position as they approached a marriageable age, and it is not surprising that both ran into difficulties at this time. Both would be subject to political pressures, and to the machinations of parents and foster parents' ambitions for their daughters, or for political power.

In 964, when Edgar was about twenty-one years old, he married the partner of his life, his queen consort Elfthrith, daughter of Ordgar, ealdorman of the Western provinces, Dorset, Somerset and Devon. Elfthrith, a lady of high rank, was already a widow of two years' duration when she married the king. Her former husband was Ethelwold, ealdorman of East Anglia who had been Edgar's close friend and kinsman, and who was also thought to have been his foster brother. Elfthrith was the first lady known to have been anointed as queen in England, since Judith, Alfred's young stepmother, was anointed queen of Wessex in her own country of France, after her marriage with Alfred's father in 856.

Elfthrith was associated with her husband in the practical aspects of the *Regularis Concordia* the new monastic rule and eccelesiastial reform. Edgar is mentioned in the preface of this great code as protector of the monasteries of the realm, and he commits to his queen the guardianship of the houses for women.

Elfthrith gave Edgar two sons, the elder, Edmund, died in 971. The younger son, Ethelred, later succeeded his half brother Edward as king of England. He is known to us as 'Ethelred the Unready'.

The highly coloured tales mostly derived from ballads probably invented long after Edgar's death, and related at length by William of Malmesbury, at least a century and a half later, may or may not have some foundation. They are supposed to relate to the period before his marriage to Elfthrith, that is before he was twenty-one. Nineteenth-century historians either doubt or refute these tales. Most historians of this century ignore them altogether. The evidence is considered to be too unreliable.

Whatever mistakes Edgar may have made in his early years can never detract from the high regard, honour and respect he earned for himself in Britain, and on the continent, throughout the years of his maturity.

The well known nineteenth-century historian Dr. W. Stubbs mentions that Canute's opinion of Edgar was not a flattering one,[13] but does not supply any contemporary evidence to substantiate this statement, which might well explain where ballads unfavourable to Edgar originated. Canute's own marriage arrangements were, to say the least, highly unorthodox. Apart from this, a Danish king on the English throne might not be unwilling to hear ballads detrimental to one of the most illustrious members of the late royal house being sung in his court.

CHAPTER FOUR

The Monastic Revival of the Tenth Century

The Viking invasions of the ninth and tenth centuries had destroyed monastic life throughout the whole of eastern England where monasteries had been sacked and destroyed and their inhabitants dispersed or slain. In fact the treasure housed in the monasteries near the east coast of England was the main objective of the earliest Viking raids.

Throughout the rest of the country scholarship and learning had been disrupted and no regular rule of life was being observed. The Benedictine rule introduced into England in the late seventh century was no longer in force. Monks everywhere had been gradually replaced by secular clergy, so that when Alfred founded a monastery at Athelney in the late ninth century there were no English monks ready to live there. Monasteries in Wessex, and West Mercia, had survived as houses of clerks or secular clergy, among them Glastonbury, Bath and Malmesbury.

Alfred and Athelstan had both made valiant efforts towards the restoration of learning and literature, but Alfred's few years of peace though well spent in this direction were not enough to make any lasting effect. Athelstan's energies, when he ruled for twelve years over an England at peace, were too heavily engaged in welding together the peoples of England into one united nation for him to make any real progress in the restoration of monasticism and learning. It is for his statesmanship, his great councils or national assemblies, and his influence on European affairs that the powerful Athelstan is best remembered.

It was at Glastonbury, where Dunstan and Ethelwold were educated and trained, that the revival of monasticism and learning began in the tenth century. Dunstan was a native of Somerset, born at Baltonsborough only a few miles from Glastonbury. His installation as abbot of Glastonbury by King Edmund prepared the way for reform. A similar movement had been in process on the continent

27

since Athelstan's time and must have influenced the English reformers. Dunstan spent at least a year in Ghent, and Oswald, the third of the great reformers, had received instruction at Fleury, and it was from these two seats of learning that scholars were invited to assist Ethelwold and his two colleagues, and other English prelates under Edgar's chairmanship, to draw up the new monastic rule the *Regularis Concordia* in the year 970.

In the decade preceding the institution of *Regularis Concordia* which took place at Winchester, a massive task of rebuilding and reform faced the three great prelates: Dunstan who became archbishop of Canterbury before the end of 960, Ethelwold, abbot of Abingdon who became bishop of Winchester in 963, and Oswald, bishop of Worcester in 960 and later archbishop of York as well. They worked throughout in complete harmony with a singularity of purpose and with the enthusiastic support and patronage of the king and queen. "From whatever impulse it may have come— tradition traced it back to the sight of a ruined abbey in his boyhood —the ambition to restore the derelict monasteries of England was a dominant interest in Edgar's life."[14]

Dunstan with his duties as archbishop of Canterbury and chief adviser to the king, was not able to take such an active part in the restoration as the other two. He was responsible for the reform and enlargement of Glastonbury, Bath, and Malmesbury, and possibly Westminster. Ethelwold was very active. He rebuilt Winchester, Abingdon, Ely, Thorney, and Peterborough and others. Oswald founded Westbury on Trym, Bristol with a school for boys and Ramsey. Worcester, Winchcombe, and others were restored by him.

And while these new centres of learning were being opened up again in the Midlands and the South, bishop Ethelwold at the king's request, drew up a rule of life to be followed in these houses. The *Regularis Concordia* was based on the Benedictine rule, but it was brought up-to-date and adapted to suit English customs and way of life in the tenth century. General ecclesiastical reforms were also incorporated into the great code.

The king and queen asked Ethelwold, who was in effect the author of the *Regularis Concordia*, to translate this Benedictine rule, which was written in Latin, the language of the church and of scholars (of whom there were so few in the tenth century England) into English, so that monks who knew no Latin would understand it. When this task was

completed Edgar and his queen rewarded Ethelwold with the manor
of Sudbourne in Suffolk as they had promised so to do.

A former dean of Wells, a distinguished historian, sums up the
importance of the *Regularis Concordia*:

"The effect of this Code in the unification of England under Edgar
and Dunstan is deserving of the historian's consideration. That
unification was the glory of Edgar's reign; it was the issue of complete
co-operation between the Church and the State, and to Dunstan
more than any other the credit must be given".[15]

The dean's last sentence shows perhaps a little bias in favour of
the great archbishop, the great man of Somerset birth. Dunstan was
the leader of the reform movement and the king's adviser, but these
dedicated colleagues Ethelwold of Winchester and Oswald of
Worcester and York should receive equal recognition for their part
in this great work. It is as well to have this reminder that, although
the political unification of England had been a slow process over the
centuries, completed by his great ancestors, inherited and preserved
by Edgar, the ecclesiastical reform and the unity of Church and
State which took place during Edgar's sovereignty was due to the
combined efforts of these three great prelates, and the enthusiastic
support of a great king. That greatest of all English kings, Alfred,
who loved learning so much, and who tried so hard to establish
scholars in his native Wessex, would have been justifiably proud of
the achievements of his great grandson.

The full effect of the work of these great reformers was not immediately apparent. The growth of scholarship (and schools of learning)
resulting from the monastic revival only reached its peak in the next
generation, but the importance of this aspect of the reformation
of the tenth century, the literature and learning associated with it,
cannot be too strongly emphasised.

CHAPTER FIVE

King Making

It is generally assumed that the Anglo-Saxons brought with them to this country their ancient Teutonic traditions of which the election of a king with hereditary title, to be their ruler, the ruler of their own particular tribe, race, or small kingdom, appears to have been an important one.

Almost all the ruling families of the eleven or twelve small kingdoms established in this country by the Anglo-Saxons in the seventh century had attempted somehow or other to trace their ancestry back to a ancient hero, or god called Woden. In the eighth century when genealogies were well established, the powerful Royal House of Mercia claimed to have the most ancient lineage, not only in this country, but in most of north west Europe, for they traced their line back to an heroic fourth-century king of the Angles in their continental kingdom. His name was Offa of Angle, and some of his legendary heroic deeds are mentioned in the ancient Anglo-Saxon poem 'Widsith'. The powerful eighth-century king, Offa of Mercia, was probably named after his famous ancestor. Edgar could trace his ancestry back to the Royal Mercian House through his great grandmother, Ealswith, wife of King Alfred, and daughter of a lady of this same royal house.

If these genealogies are correct, our present monarch, who can claim descent from Edgar, and from the founder of the Royal House of Wessex, can also claim descent from the great Mercian kings, and from the ancient continental king, Offa of Angle.

Until the late eighth century the inauguration of an Anglo-Saxon king seems to have been an exclusively secular occasion, celebrated perhaps by a great banquet, possibly by an enthronement, or an investiture with royal insignia and acclamation by the great men of the kingdom.

It has been suggested that, the magnificent helmet, the so-called sceptre and standard, found on the Sutton Hoo burial site (a ship) not far from Woodbridge in Suffolk in the late 1930s, were the insignia of royalty of a seventh-century East Anglian king. These treasures may now be seen in the British Museum. Crowns were probably not worn in this country until the ninth century.

The first Anglo-Saxon king known to have been inaugurated with ecclesiastical rites was the son of that same great king, Offa of Mercia, whose name is remembered today only because he built the great boundary between England and Wales known as Offa's Dyke. Possibly influenced by continental customs, Offa, who was in close touch with Charlemagne and his court, decided that his son Ecgfrith should be consecrated king of Mercia in 787, so that his succession should be assured. Offa regarded himself, and signed himself as 'Ruler of all the English' at this time.

Nothing is known with certainty about King Ecgfrith's consecration, nor about those of his successors. Papal legates were in England in 786 and 787, but whether they attended or officiated at the ceremony, which was thought to have been held at Chelsea, is a matter for conjecture. Offa was the sort of king who would do nothing by halves, but how Ecgfrith was consecrated, and if he was anointed on the head by the new archbishop of Lichfield, or the papal legates, remains an open question.

In Northumbria about ten years later a king was crowned with ecclesiastical rites, but there is no contemporary evidence to describe how that consecration was carried out.

There is no mention of consecration in connection with the Wessex kings until after Alfred's time. The *Chronicle* records one king after another as "―――― succeeded to the kingdom".

Athelstan was consecrated according to the *Chronicle* at Kingston-on-Thames in 925, and so were his successors, although King Edmund's consecration is not mentioned. There were good reasons why Alfred's descendants should seek consecration at their inauguration to kingship. Alfred's predecessor and older brother, King Ethelred, left sons one of whom appears to have contested Edward the Elder's right to succeed King Alfred. Although there is no mention of it, Athelstan's father may have been the first Wessex king to seek consecration in order to strengthen his position as Alfred's elected heir, or to protect his successors.

Athelstan, of all Wessex kings, was most highly regarded and sought after on the continent and it is not surprising to find that he followed the continental practice of being consecrated by the church upon his election.

It now seems reasonably certain that all tenth-century English kings were anointed.

Comparison with continental procedures is interesting. Frankish kings in the eighth century were anointed, usually by the Pope himself, as patrons and protectors of the Church of Rome. Pippin, Charlemagne's father, was the first, and archbishop Boniface then bishop of Mayence the great Wessex missionary to pagan North West Europe, who with his Anglo-Saxon colleagues had converted Germany and united the Frankish Church and State, consecrated Pippin at Soissins. Pippin and his two sons were all anointed by the Pope himself a few years later. After his brother's death, Charlemagne became sole ruler of the Frankish kingdom, and was finally crowned in Rome by the Pope, in the year 800, as Roman Emperor.

From Pippin's time it became the custom of Frankish Carolingian, kings that the heir or heirs to the kingdom should be crowned and anointed during the father's lifetime, so that the succession would be assured.

After the breakup of the great Carolingian Empire, in the year 887, the German (Saxon) Emperors became the patrons and protectors of the Church of Rome and were anointed by the Pope. Edgar's uncle by marriage, Otto the First, was the first German Emperor to be anointed by Rome. Henry, his father, had refused to be anointed but had accepted kingship and the protectorate. The Ottonians, as they were called, also followed the custom of anointing and crowning the heir to the empire, during his father's lifetime.

A second coronation and anointing was not an unusual occurence with either the Carolingians or the Ottonians. For example, both Pippin and Otto II were twice anointed.

There are some parallels to be drawn between events in England and the continent at these times.

King Pippin's coronation with anointing followed the unification of the Frankish Church and State, brought about by the mission and efforts of Boniface and his Anglo-Saxon colleagues. Boniface whose Saxon name was Wynfrith was a Wessex nobleman, born west of Selwood, educated at Exeter, and for some time head of the monastic school at Nursling near Southampton.

The unification of Germany under the Ottonians, after the breakup of the Carolingian Empire in 887, was followed by monastic and ecclesiastical reform on the continent and was contemporary with the unification of England followed by monastic and ecclesiastic reform under the kings of Wessex. Archbishop Dunstan, also a native of Wessex, was the leader of this reformation and was also to a great extent the organiser of the Bath coronation and anointing.

That the Bath coronation in 973 was different from any previous ceremony of its kind in this country seems apparent from the emphasis given to it by the *Saxon Chronicler* and other near contemporary writers. But, since Edgar's was the first coronation and anointing of an English king to be described and recorded there is no basis for comparison. At the present time it is only possible to make assumptions. The most reasonable assumption seems to be that Edgar was not indeed the first king of all England, he was the first lord (emperor) of the whole of Britain, and that he was acclaimed, or elected, not only by the Saxons, Mercians and Northumbrians, but also by the princes or leaders of every race or people living in Britain, and on the islands around its coast.

The chart on page 34 illustrates the continental influences on English king-making.

The Franks (Carolingians)	*Consecrated as king*	*Imperial Coronation*
EIGHTH CENTURY		
Pippin, king of the Franks	A.D. 751 By Boniface of Wessex	
Sons of Pippin Charles (Charlemagne) Caroloman (died 771)	A.D. 754 Pippin and sons anointed by Pope Stephen	A.D. 800 Charlemagne
Sons of Charlemagne Pippin Louis	A.D. 781 By Pope Hadrian	
England Son of King Offa Ecgfrith of Mercia A.D. 787	Possibly in the presence of Papal Legates	
The Germans TENTH CENTURY Otto I Otto II	A.D. 936 A.D. 959 (sole emperor)	A.D. 962 A.D. 967 A.D. 973
The English TENTH CENTURY Athelstan of England Edmund „ Edred „ Edwig „ Edgar „	A.D. 925 A.D. 939 A.D. 946 A.D. 955 King of Mercia and Northumbria A.D. 957 and Wessex A.D. 959	K. of England Lord (emperor) of Britain A.D. 973

Although the relations between England and Germany were close and friendly during Edgar's reign, there was no East Frankish (German) influence on the coronation order drawn up by archbishop Dunstan. Throughout the tenth century the English coronation ritual was derived from West Frankish (Carolingian) and Biblical sources.

The Coronation Order

An 'order' in the sense here used is: The prescribed form for the performance of a ceremony (of the Church) or, the administration of a religious rite.

There are in existence three versions of Edgar's coronation order of 973, all of which appear to derive from a much earlier Anglo-Saxon coronation order. This early Anglo-Saxon order is thought to date back to about 900 to 925, that is roughly, Edward the Elder's reign. His son Athelstan was consecrated in 925, about a year after his father's death, so this early order could have been used for either or both these kings.

It has in the past been mistakenly considered as a draft for archbishop Dunstan's order of 973, but it is now known with certainty to be early tenth century and mainly of West Frankish origin, and some of its prayer texts are thought to go back to the first half of the ninth century. So far nothing is known of its use in this country except that all three versions of the 973 order derive from it. These are:

1. The S.M.N. Order: so-called because Saxons, Mercians, and Northumbrians are mentioned in the consecration prayer. Dunstan is thought to have revised one version of this S.M.N. Order for the consecration of 973, and this became known as:
2. The Edgar Order used at the Bath coronation.
3. The Fulrad Order.

This appears to be a copy of the Anglo-Saxon order supposedly made by Fulrad, a West Frankish prelate and a friend of Dunstan's. There is no evidence to suggest that it was ever used.

Dunstan's revised version of this early tenth-century English coronation order was used at the Bath coronation and has since been referred to as the Edgar Order. Copies of this order occur in several manuscripts of the late tenth and early eleventh centuries, with some variations, and since most of these are accompanied by an order for a queen's consecration, it is assumed that Edgar's consort Elfthrith was also crowned and anointed in 973.

The Queen's Order used in 973 is copied from the order for a West Frankish queen of about A.D. 900 whose companion order for a king was one of the main sources used for the early tenth-century Anglo-Saxon order, the S.M.N. text. An earlier order for the coronation of an English queen exists. It is a West Frankish order used for the coronation of Judith,* Alfred's young stepmother, whose coronation took place after her marriage to King Ethelwulf of Wessex in the church at Verberie-sur-Oise, when Ethelwulf married her on his way home from Rome in the year 856. This order was not used again.

Dunstan's Order for the Bath coronation provided for:

Anointing, as for a bishop of the Church, and
Investiture with crown and ring.

In tenth-century England, according to Schramm, continental influences on coronation procedures were very apparent:

The oath of the subject,
The promise of the king,
The investiture with regalia

were all signs of the connection with the continent and its development.

It might be well to add here, and Schramm infers this:

England is influenced by the continent, and has been so influenced down through the centuries. She adopts continental styles and customs in an individual way, not blindly following a fashion. The English have taken a style or fashion from Europe in the past and, whether it be architectural, legal, monetary, or ceremonial, they have 'Anglicised' it and made it in a peculiar way their own. This is more apparent to the nations of Europe than it is to the English themselves, and this is what happened to Edgar's coronation order. Its subsequent history is interesting:

England: Soon after the Norman conquest, although two or three of its prayer texts were retained, Dunstan's coronation order, was replaced by an official order of the Church of Rome which was mainly of German origin.

France: Probably sometime in the eleventh century the S.M.N. version of the Edgar order was adopted as the official French coronation order, and it remained so as long as the French monarchy survived.

The beautiful coronation book of 1365 made for Charles V, king of France, which contains the order used for his magnificent coronation in 1364, actually mentions 'Saxons, Mercians, and Northumbrians', in the consecration prayer! It would be interesting to know if the officiating

*Daughter of Charles the Bald, King of the Western Franks.

archbishop actually read out these strange words, he probably did, who would notice?

As late as 1825, the oath which Charles X of France took was, in all essentials, the same as that which had been drafted for Edgar in 973. In English it reads:

"In the name of the Holy Trinity I promise three things to the Christian people my subjects:

first: that God's Church and all Christian people of my realm shall enjoy true peace;

second: that I forbid all ranks of men, robbery and all wrongful deeds;

third: that I urge and command justice and mercy in all judgements, so that the Gracious and Compassionate God who lives and reigns may grant us all His everlasting mercy."

Hungary: The Edgar order became the basis for the Hungarian coronation rite.

Normandy: The Dukes of Normandy also used Dunstan's order as the basis of their inauguration ceremony.

Jerusalem: Lastly, the French order was adopted by the kingdom of Jerusalem.

Thus, Edgar's coronation order has not only been in use for a thousand years (in Europe) but has also been imported by another continent.[16]

The Coronation

There exists a near contemporary account of the Bath coronation on the 11th of May 973. It is described as an eye witness's account although it was not actually recorded until about twenty-two years later.

It begins by recording that bishops, abbots, nobles and secular magnates assembled in Bath for the festival, and then describes the procession to the church where nobles, lay magnates and the people awaited the king.

Edgar went to the church in an ecclesiastical procession of abbots, abbesses, bishops, and clergy.

"Two bishops led him to the church walking one on either hand and chanting the antiphon 'Firmetur manus tua' (Ps. lxxxviii. 14).

"He wore his crown, but laid it aside before the high altar. As he did so archbishop Dunstan began the *Te Deum*, which was sung by the multitude of monks and clergy.

"When the hymn was ended two bishops raised the king from the ground and, at the dictation of Dunstan, he took a threefold oath,
>   To guard the church of God,
>   To forbid Violence and Wrong,
>   And to keep Justice, Judgement, and Mercy.

"Dunstan then made a prayer and this was followed by a prayer pronounced by Oswald archbishop of York.

"After this the king was anointed, the full voiced choir singing the antiphon which tells how Zadok the priest and Nathan the prophet anointed Solomon king in Zion (1 Kings, i. 45).

"Then Dunstan placed a ring on the king's hand,
>   girt him with a sword, put the crown upon his head,
>   and gave him his blessing.

"Edgar also received the sceptre and the rod, and lastly the mass was sung, 'The glories of the day' . . . ."[17]

The English chronicler concerned himself more with the ritual, which was of early Frankish origin, than with a description of the scene.

The description of the coronation of Otto the First by the German writer Widukind is much more vivid and colourful, but omits the details of the German ritual.

"Leading Otto to the front of the (chapel or throne room over the) Cathedral porch at Aix (la Chapelle) the archbishop of Mayence addressed the assembled multitude in the following words: 'I bring you the elect of God, the successor designated by his father, Henry, Now made king by all the princes. If the choice please you, hold up your hands'; and every hand was raised with acclamation in confirmation of the election.

"Otto, clad in a short tunic, after the Frank fashion, was then conducted into the church, and invested at the altar with the insignia of royalty—the sword and belt, the robe and bracelets, the sceptre, staff, and diadem—and then anointed with holy oil by the metropolitan of Germany. And wearing the golden diadem, he was again led into (the chapel over) the porch by the archbishop of Mayence and Cologne, and placed upon the throne in sight of all the people."[18]

This chapel, or throne room, over the porch at Aix or Aachen, would be in the west tower of the great palace chapel completed by Charlemagne about the year A.D. 800 which is still the cathedral of that city.

The tower had three stages, or storeys—a porch on ground floor level—a 'kaiserhalle or throne room on the first floor—and a treasury on the third stage. Staircase turrets to the north and south of the tower gave access to the king's chapel or throne room, and to the treasury above. The king's throne would normally face eastwards to an altar at Tribune, or first floor level, but on this occasion, presumably, the throne was placed to face a large open window to the west, to allow the people outside the church to see their newly enthroned sovereign in full regalia.

Such upper west chapels similar to, but not so grand as that at Aachen, were built in England before Charlemagne adopted this fashion on the continent. Examples of these royal chapels, as they often were in this country, contemporary with, and in the first case, even earlier than Aachen, were built over west porches, now heightened to become western towers, at Deerhurst in Gloucestershire, and at Brixworth in Northants. They are still to be seen in these churches.

In tenth-century England, as on the continent, the west porch was often heightened to become a west tower, and in the larger churches this tower would be flanked by porches or chapels to become a 'westwork'.

It would be interesting to know that Edgar in 973, like his uncle at Aachen in 936, had shown himself in his coronation regalia from the upper floor of a westwork of Bath Abbey to all his subjects waiting without.

He probably did. In fact the suitability of the westwork at Bath might well have been another reason for having the coronation ceremony in the recently enlarged church.

The Coronation Banquet

From all accounts there was nothing the Anglo-Saxons enjoyed more than a good banquet, unless it was dressing themselves up for such an occasion.

The great banquet which took place in Bath on the day of Edgar's coronation must have been a memorable occasion. The early chronicler has little to say about this part of the ceremony.

The king with his ealdormen and attendants made their way to
the great hall of the palace. Of the clergy, only the archbishops of
York and Canterbury seated on either side of the king, as guests of
honour, were mentioned. About them sat the great ealdormen of the
country, most of them kinsmen of the king. Schramm suggests that a
'skald' or bard would be present to sing of the heroic deeds of the king
and his ancestors.[19]

According to ancient tradition special services would be rendered
to the king during the course of this banquet, one noble offering a
dish, another a cup, a third held his sword, and so on. Nobles performed
these services at the coronation of Teutonic kings to show their
willingness to be regarded as his men.

Meanwhile in another hall nearby the queen, Elfthrith, who was
also crowned and anointed in 973, with crown and ring, acted as
hostess, presumably, to abbots and abbesses and bishops too. In earlier
times feasting and banqueting might go on for two or three days, but
the presence of the great ecclesiastics must have changed the character
and added greater dignity to these occaions.

When the feasting and celebrations in Bath were at an end, it is
recorded that King Edgar set sail in his fleet and arrived at Chester,
where he was met by six or eight subject kings, of the Welsh, the
Scots, and of the islands off the coasts of Britain:

"973. And immediately after that the king took his whole naval
force to Chester, and six kings came to meet him, and all gave him
pledges that they would be his allies on sea and on land", says the
Anglo-Saxon chronicler."

A later source, Florence of Worcester, considered reliable in this,
says:

"... and his eight sub-kings, namely Kenneth, king of the Scots,
Malcolm, king of the Cumbrians, Maccus, king of many islands,
and five others, Dufnal (Dunmail), Siferth, Hywel, Jacob (Iago),
and Juchil, met him as he commanded, and swore that they would
be faithful to him, and be his allies by land and sea.

"And on a certain day he went on board a boat with them, and
with them at the oars, and himself seizing the helm, he steered it
skilfully on the course of the river Dee, proceeding from the palace
to the monastery of St. John the Baptist, attended by all the crowd
of ealdormen and nobles, also by boat. And when he had completed

his prayers he returned with the same pomp to the palace. As he entered he is reported to have said to his nobles, that any of his successors might indeed pride himself on being king of the English, when he might have the glory of such honours, with so many kings subservient to him."[20]

This ceremony, of rowing King Edgar on the river Dee, by the six or eight Celtic and Norse rulers, is considered to be similar in purpose to the special services rendered to Edgar by his nobles at the coronation banquet. It was an act of recognition by these rulers of Edgar's sovereignty. They were, in this way, showing their allegiance and submission to their elected overlord, and Lord (emperor) of Britain.

The Coronation City

One reason why Bath was chosen as the place of Edgar's coronation ceremony was its position. The river Avon at Bath had for centuries been the boundary between the two great rival kingdoms of Mercia and Wessex. Anglo-Saxon kings liked to meet on a boundary between kingdoms to make peace treaties, sign charters, or discuss affairs of importance. Bath was just such a meeting place. Kingston-on-Thames which King Athelstan had chosen for his coronation was another.

Bath was also a great road centre. The ancient trade and military routes from Northumbria and the Midlands to the Mendips, and from the Thames valley to the Severn estuary, all passed through Bath, which was only a short distance from the Severn estuary. From this estuary, or more probably from the river Avon at Bath (navigable until recent times) King Edgar and his court, as soon as the Bath celebrations were ended, sailed to Chester, another border city, accompanied by the entire naval force of Britain.

The city, with its monastery and its dependent manors, had, in about 781, become part of the personal (hereditary) estates of the Mercian Royal House,[21] whose rulers not only recognised the importance of its border position and accessibility, but probably liked it for its amenities—its delightful position, surrounded as it was then, only by green hills and woodlands. Its hot springs, were an added attraction throughout the city's history. The royal palace at Bath probably dated from that time.

During the Danish invasion of the ninth century, King Alfred was obliged to make Bath one of his fortresses, because of its strategic

position as a gateway from Mercia into Wessex. In his time, the old
Roman walls would have been repaired, and the ditch around them
cleaned and deepened. That Alfred restored the city walls was an
ancient tradition in Bath. If the list of fortresses drawn up in the reign
of Alfred's son, Edward the Elder, is to be relied on, Bath, for its size,
must have been the most heavily manned fortress in the country.

Although there is no record of Bath, the royal Mercian city, being
taken over by Wessex, there is little doubt that it became a Wessex
city in Alfred's reign.   He may have asked for it of his son-in-law
Ethelred of Mercia as part of his defensive scheme, but it is more
likely that he acquired it through his queen, whose mother was a
lady of the royal Mercian House. That Bath became a Wessex city
from Alfred's time is shown by its appearance on charters as such.

Edgar and Dunstan had restored and enlarged the old church at
Bath, and had established the Benedictine rule in the monastery,
which may also have needed restoration or rebuilding. The Saxon
church occupied part of the site of the present church, but extended
farther eastwards: to the west it probably did not reach much farther
than the present tower and transepts.

The monastery was immediately south of the church. The royal
palace, it will be shown, was well to the south west. Edgar may have
enlarged the palace buildings, or may have added a new hall with
outbuildings and extra bowers (chambers) for the great occasion.

The small city would lack the accommodation needed for all the
people who were invited, or who wished to watch the coronation
procession and to see the great king in his regalia. Many of the sight-
seers would arrive with their tents and equipment, and the city would
probably be surrounded by bustling camps.

Towards the end of the tenth century, Bath, in area and overall
plan differed only in detail from the city shown on Speed's map at
the end of the sixteenth century. It lay within its Roman walls, a small
city occupying no more than twenty-five acres. The position of its
three hot springs, and of the monastery and palace, allowed little
scope for changes in layout. Probably it was because of the space needed
for monastery and palace that the old Roman street plan had to a
great extent been lost. The city centre it seems was at the north end
of Stall Street where there appears to have been an open space.

Apart from the churches and the city walls, all the buildings of
the city would be of timber construction with roofs of thatch. It is

possible that the royal hall at Bath may have been of stone, or part stone construction, but, until the late sixteenth century, a stone dwelling house was a rarity in Bath. Alfred in the late ninth century, according to Asser his biographer, "erected royal halls and chambers with stone and wood". We also know, thanks to an awful accident* which occurred at Calne in Wiltshire in the late tenth century, that halls of two storeys were not unusual, although it may have been that the council chamber only was on the upper floor. This type of building it seems was common in Bath, and elsewhere, after the conquest. But pre-conquest domestic buildings are usually described as of one storey only.

Edgar and his brother, King Edwig, seemed to know Bath well, and both were generous benefactors to the monastery. Edwig, in the preamble to one of his grants to the monastery of Bath, described the church of St. Peter as the abbey was then known, as "a most remarkable building". In another preamble he mentions that "pleasant warm baths are taken from the hot springs". King Edwig gave Bathampton, Tiden-ham, Weston, Cold Ashton, and possibly other places, to St. Peter's, Bath, while Edgar was still with him at his court. Edgar's attestation as witness is on these charters of 956 and 957.

The Royal Palace at Bath

There are good reasons for suggesting that the royal Saxon palace at Bath was on the site later occupied by the first bishop of Bath, John of Tours. William Rufus who handed over, or sold, the city and monastery of Bath to this bishop in the year 1090, says in his charter:

"Know that I have given to God and St. Peter in Bath, and to John the bishop, the whole city of Bath in alms and for the augmentation of the episcopal see, and to all his successors . . . I have given him freely and gratuitously *with all appurtenances which I had there, or my father in happier days* . . . so that he may have his episcopal seat there with the greatest honour."[22]

There exists ample evidence of the site and extent of bishop John's palace and its enclosure. Its boundary wall enclosed most of the area we now see as the Roman Baths site. The medieval stalls or shops in

---

*"978 in this year all the chief councillors of the English people fell from an upper storey at Calne, except that Archbishop Dunstan alone remained standing on a beam; and some were severely injured there, and some did not survive it."—*Anglo-Saxon Chronicle.*

Stall Street backed on to the wall of the courtyard of the bishop's palace on either side of the entrance gate. Bishop John's massive fortress-like palace with its stone keep or tower, built to withstand siege, was obsolete by the mid-thirteenth century, and probably by the end of that century was used for other purposes. John Leland, who visited Bath in the 1530s mentioned John of Tours' palace:

"This John of Tours erectid a palace at Bath in the south west of the monasteri at St. Peter's at Bath: one gret squar tour of it with other ruins yet appere."

According to the city archives the ruins of this old palace were pulled down in 1569. In the meantime the thirteenth-century bishops, who had their palace in Wells, had built for themselves a more suitable residence in the Bath palace enclosure, well away from the old palace, towards the east of the site. Like the royal Saxon palaces on this site, it was used as a place of occasional residence, and in the fourteenth century bishop Ralph gave this later wing, with that part of the land adjoining the house within the palace walls, 170 by 130 feet, to the prior of the monastery, "reserving to the bishop and his successor's the use of such dwelling when they should come to Bath."[23] The bishop's house, which became known as the Prior's Lodging, survived the dissolution of the monastery, having in the meantime been much altered and enlarged. It was not pulled down until the year 1755. There is evidence that the old Norman palace hall, one wall of which was parallel to Stall Street and almost in line with the eastern end of the present King's Bath, was used as a mill building. In the early eighteenth century, a millstone was dug up in the garden of a house on the site. In the late nineteenth century it was decided that an ancient sluice from the King's Bath, found during excavations and repairs, had been used in connection with a mill near the Stall Street end of the site.

The director of excavations of the Roman Baths site during the 1870s to the 1890s made occasional references to the Saxon palace of which he had found evidence, but he left no records. He also suggested that the wall surrounding the Roman Baths was to a great extent used as the foundations for the walls of the Saxon palace enclosure which he dates back to the eighth century. In the absence of concrete evidence little weight can be given to these statements. One suggestion that does seem possible of proof today, is that the palace enclosure which appears to have ended westwards by a wall only two or three yards to the west of the present King's Bath, would have been almost identical, not with the Roman bathing establishment of the fourth or fifth century, but with that area of it which we can see today. In which case the foundations of its walls might to some extent have been used.

Saxon 'palaces' were places of occasional residence for the itinerant king and his court, although some distant kinsman of the king, a steward, or reeve, would live permanently in one of these palaces. Alfred, the military reeve of Bath whose death the Anglo-Saxon chronicler records in the year A.D. 906, probably lived in the palace at Bath.

A palace much favoured by Edgar's father and uncles was that of Cheddar in Somerset, where recent excavations have recovered the layout, probably similar to that we might expect to find in Saxon Bath. Within the Cheddar palace enclosure, the postholes of several large oblong 'halls' of different dates were found. There were also several ancillary buildings or 'bowers', chapels of different periods, built on the same site, and a mill.[24] In this part of the country, royal Saxon palaces have been recorded at: Frome, Chippenham, Pucklechurch, and Warminster. Cheddar was popular because of the deer hunting possibilities in the neighbourhood, and a vast area of royal parkland lay to the south of Bath with similar facilities.

The King's Bath almost certainly gets its name from its position within the palace enclosure. It has been rebuilt since the Saxon kings bathed in it, but the name probably goes back to the eighth century (as the nineteenth-century excavator suggested). It was late in this century that Bath became a royal hereditary estate, and the engineering skill of that period, which won the admiration of the late Sir Cyril Fox,[25] may also have enabled the powerful Mercian king who owned Bath at that time to have a fine bath built for him on this site.

The nineteenth-century excavator seems to have had the idea that the Saxons used the reservoirs of the three hot springs for the purpose of bathing. This would not have been a very enjoyable experience, with water bubbling up at about 120° F.

Bede, who wrote in the first half of the eighth century, mentioned that people bathed in the hot springs, separately, according to age and sex. He does not mention Bath specifically, but it is difficult to associate any other place in England with this statement.

Nennius, in the ninth century, goes a step farther, and mentions as one of the marvels of Britain, for he was of British descent, a warm pool surrounded by a stone wall where men go to wash. He goes on to say that if a man wishes for cold water, the pool will be cold, and if he wishes for warm water it will be warm. Except for the washing, he might well be describing one of the treatment baths of today!

CHAPTER SIX

Edgar's Death, and After

King Edgar died suddenly in July 975, little more than two years after his Bath coronation:

"975. In this year died Edgar, ruler of the Angles, friend of the West Saxons, and protector of the Mercians. It was widely known throughout many nations across the gannet's bath (English Channel) that king's honoured Edmund's son far and wide, and paid homage to this king as was his due by birth. Nor was there fleet so proud nor host so strong that it got itself prey in England as long as the noble king held the throne."

"In his day things improved greatly, and God granted him that he lived in peace as long as he lived; and, as was necessary for him, he laboured zealously for this; he exalted God's praise far and wide, and loved God's law; and he improved the peace of the people more than kings who were before him in the memory of man ... kings and earls willingly submitted to him and were subjected to whatever he wished. And without battle he brought under his sway all that he wished ... and he continually and frequently directed all his people wisely in matters of Church and State. Yet he did one ill-deed too greatly: He loved evil foreign customs and brought too firmly heathen manners within this land, and attracted hither foreigners and enticed harmful people to this country. But may God grant him that his good deeds may prove greater than his ill-deeds, for the protection of his soul on its everlasting journey."

Thus, the *Anglo-Saxon Chronicle* reviews the reign of the last of the truly great kings of the House of Wessex. The second of the two extracts is thought to have been written by archbishop Wulfstan of York in the early eleventh century. Its curious and enigmatic ending defies explanation, except that Wulfstan was to the Anglo-Saxons, as Gildas was to the Britons, a prophet of doom, of disaster through their own misdeeds. Gildas in the sixth century railed against the lax morality and the plurality of wives of the British princes, but what evil foreign customs and people, Edgar, 'who loved God's law' introduced into this country, unless it was his three attempts at matrimony, may always remain an unsolved mystery. It may be just an example of Wulfstan's 'early English insularity', or it may have been written in Canute's reign.

King Edgar was laid to rest by the side of his father Edmund in Glastonbury abbey. The son of his first wife Ethelfled, Edward, a boy of about fifteen, succeeded his father after a period of violent dispute verging on civil war. King Edward was consecrated at Kingston by archbishop Dunstan before the end of 975, but many would have preferred Ethelred the younger son of Edgar, and of his queen Elfthrith. In some ways perhaps this was a situation similar to that of 957 when the country divided against Edgar's brother. This time the opposing factions did not resolve their differences so easily as in 957. King Edward was brutally murdered in 978 by some of his young half-brothers' retainers near Corfe Castle in Dorset as he was on his way to visit his brother and step-mother in residence there. Because of this terrible death he was afterwards known as Edward the Martyr. Ethelred, who was only a boy of eleven or twelve, at this time could have had no part in those awful events.

Edward was hastily buried at Wareham in Dorset, but a year later he was given a more suitable resting place in Shaftesbury Abbey.

Queen Elfthrith's son Ethelred (the Unready) was consecrated by archbishop Dunstan about a month after his stepbrother's death. The boy king's mother became the third queen mother, with the party surrounding her, to rule the kingdom within a period of about forty years.

There is a rather sad connection between these two brothers and Bradford-on-Avon:

"Ethelred in the year 1001 bestowed on the church of St. Edward (at Shaftesbury) the vill and monastery of Bradford, Wiltshire, to be subject to the nuns, that, with the relics of King Edward the Blessed Martyr (his brother), and other saints, they might find there a refuge ('impenetrable confugium') against the attacks of the Danes, the king stipulating that: on the restoration of peace and tranquility, when the sisters returned to their ancient home, they should leave behind them at Bradford, a sufficient community, according as the prior should think fit, for its monastic state to be maintained."[26]

It is possible that Ethelred intended that the refuge of the Shaftesbury nuns would be the forest of Selwood, part of which then belonged to Bradford monastery.

Peace in this land was indeed at an end when King Edgar died.

But Alfred's descendants had left behind them the peoples of England so firmly united as one nation, Edgar's inheritance, which he passed on strengthened and intact to his successors, that this nation somehow survived Danish rule, and Norman conquest, and remained an English nation. Danes and Normans over the years became 'Anglicised' and today we still call ourselves 'Anglo-Saxons' when we want to bring to notice our better qualities. More often though, we use 'British' and 'Britain' which serves as a reminder that many of our people, in Wales and Cornwall and in the far north west of England are the descendants of those Celtic inhabitants of this country who survived Roman and Anglo-Saxon conquest also, as 'the Britons'.

THE DESCENT FROM EDGAR

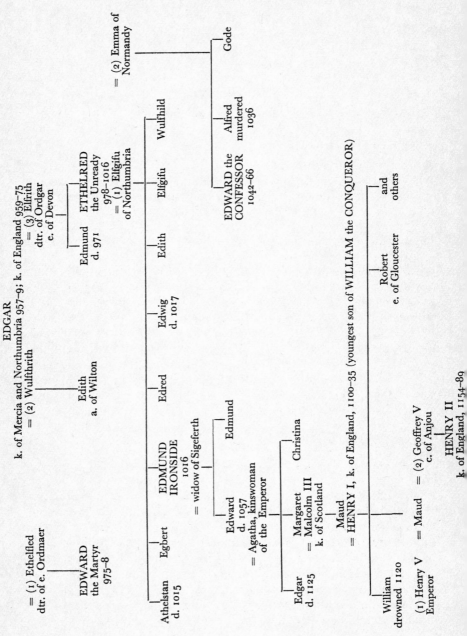

CHAPTER SEVEN

William of Malmesbury

William of Malmesbury is probably the most widely read, and in some respects, one of the most reliable of early medieval historians, if medieval historians can ever be called reliable as the term is used today. They were at their best and most useful when they were writing of the time in which they lived. When they used earlier sources for their information they would often mention this but almost invariably the source was not named.

Contemporary or near contemporary writers like Ethelweard, the king's near kinsman of exalted rank, and the monk of Ramsey who described Edgar's coronation, have nothing but praise for the two brothers. Ethelweard wrote his annals when Edgar's queen was a power in the land as the queen mother of the boy King Ethelred, and probably because of his exalted position as the leading nobleman, he was able to give only the barest outline of the two reigns.

It is from post conquest, and later writers of the twelfth century like William, that the morals of the two brothers were questioned. On this subject Dr. Stubbs, quoting Robertson, says that:

"The history of Edgar was written without regard to historical evidence or decent loyalty."

This sentence might equally have applied to Edgar's brother Edwig.

It is difficult for us, as it was for those nineteenth-century historians, to realise the limitations under which William in his monastery of Malmesbury wrote about events which happened more than a century and a half before his time. Like all historians, up to our own time he described Edgar as one of the greatest kings of his line and was very lavish with his adulation. Too lavish, because, after using all the superlatives he is able to command, he turns to the bawdy ballad stories invented in all probability more than one generation after Edgar's death, and appears to enjoy the telling of them.

Many of these stories about the two brothers have been proved unreliable as indeed William admits they might well be. William's account of the boy king, Edwig's, relations with his future queen and her mother is today too absurd to bear repetition. In fairness to William it should be mentioned that earlier post-conquest writers, Eadmer and his contemporary Osbern, have equally unbelievable stories to tell about this young king and his youthful wife. Stenton, however, points out that after Edwig's death at the age of nineteen years, both his queen and her mother moved in the highest circles and were accepted by the great prelates of the church, thus belying the truth of these legends.[27]

The accusation that Edwig was a despoiler of monasteries may have some slight foundation, but a young king whose life ended at the age of nineteen should be given the benefit of the doubt on matters of this kind. It is unlikely that Edwig ever wielded any real power in the land. King Edwig's charters show that he was as great a benefactor to the monasteries during his short and unhappy reign as any member of his house in the same number of years. Bath monastery had reason to be grateful for his generosity, and so had others. That some religious houses suffered in his time may have been due to the policy of the party ruling in his name.

Malmesbury has left a very full account of King Edgar's reign which contains factual errors as well as misjudgements: in anecdotal vein he records at length a dream that Edgar is supposed to have had during a hunting expedition and the interpretation of this dream by Edgar's mother, the lady Elfgifu. There is no doubt whatever that Elfgifu died either at Edgar's birth, or very soon after. This anecdote is obviously fictitious.

Again, according to William, Edgar killed his close friend and kinsman, Ethelwold of East Anglia, so that he could marry Ethelwold's wife Elfthrith. That this story too is a fabrication is proved by the fact that Ethelwold's death is recorded in the year 962 by a near contemporary source which does not mention Edgar in connection with it, but does mention Edgar's marriage with his friend's widow.[28] This occurred at least two years later, in 964. Further proof is shown by the disappearance of ealdorman Ethelwold's name attesting charters in the year 962, and being replaced by that of his brother Ethelwine, who remained one of the king's friends and ealdormen. Edgar in 962 was probably still involved with Wulfthrith whose daughter was born either late in 961 or early in 962. At this time also Edgar was barely nineteen years old.

Malmesbury also said:

" . . . that from the sixteenth year of his age, when he was appointed king, till the thirtieth, he reigned without the insignia of royalty."

Ethelweard, Edgar's friend and contemporary, has recorded in his chronicle Edgar's inauguration to kingship in 957 when Edgar was fourteen years old. And it was as a crowned king that Edgar came to Bath in 973, according to another near contemporary source. Is there any more to be said about the errors of William except that he was not usually so ill-informed?

'The King of Bath'

King Edgar's benefactions to the church at St. Peter's, Bath, are known and recorded. He was also known to be a great benefactor to the city, but exactly what form these benefactions took has always been a matter for speculation. It is certain that a lasting affection and gratitude kept the name of King Edgar alive, and his great coronation ceremony a part of the city's heritage down the centuries. 'The King' in Bath meant Edgar.

William of Malmesbury writing in the twelfth century said:

" . . . the transactions of his reign are celebrated with peculiar splendour (in Bath) even in our time."[29]

In the sixteenth century John Leland wrote:

"King Edgar was crounid with much joy and honor at St. Peter's in Bath: whereapon he bare a gret zeale to the towne, and gave very great frauncheses and privileges onto it. In the knowledge wherof they pray in al their ceremonies for the soule of king Eadgar. And at Whitsunday-tyde at which tyme men say that Eadgar there was crounid, there is a king elected at Bath every yere of the tounesmen in the joyfulle remembraunce of king Eadgar and the privilege gyven by hym. This king is fested and his adherents, by the richest menne of the toun."[30]

Early in the seventeenth century, during the reign of James I, a new Guildhall was built in the middle of the High street. The hall itself was on first floor level. At ground level between classical arcades was an open area for the market stallholders. On the Guildhall facade facing the main city gate (the north gate) were two niches. King Edgar's statue occupied one of them, the other statue is thought to be that of King Osric, founder of the first Saxon monastery at Bath.

These two statues, now quite unrecognisable, occupy niches on a building at the south west end of Bath Street, close to the Hot Bath.

In the early eighteenth century, when Beau Nash had managed to have himself elected as 'master of ceremonies' in Bath, this great annual 'king making' ceremony was remembered for the last time, and Richard Nash took over the traditional title of 'The King of Bath'.

Stained Glass

The most famous kings of Wessex may be seen in stained glass windows in Bath and Wells.

King Edgar's coronation is the subject of a window at the east end of the north choir aisle in Bath Abbey. The main part of this window shows Dunstan, archbishop of Canterbury, about to place the crown on Edgar's head, the king holding orb and sceptre is seated on a throne and Oswald, archbishop of York, is standing beside the king evidently assisting in the ceremony.

In the tracery of the window above this scene is an open book with a quill and presumably some sort of inkwell to go with it, which is probably intended to represent the revival of learning, made possible by the restoration of the monasteries. At the bottom of the window, underneath the coronation scene, a splendid boat rides the waves as a reminder to the onlooker that Edgar commanded the English navy most successfully.

In the north transept of the cathedral church at Wells, little more than twenty miles from Bath, where crowds gather to wait for the chimes of the ancient clock, are six of the great kings of Wessex in stained glass.

They are on the north facing windows of this north transept. All six, in chronological order and more than life size.

As one faces these windows, they are, from left to right:

Ine: The great Wessex law maker of the seventh century, builder of the first Saxon church at Glastonbury, and founder of the church of Wells.

Egbert: Descendant of Ine's brother Ingild, and Alfred's grandfather. An exile at Charlemagne's court for a few years, until he returned to England to found a line of great kings of Wessex and to become a power in the land.

Alfred the Great: The greatest English king of all time.

Edward the Elder: Alfred' son, a fighting king of Wessex.

Athelstan, here called the warrior king, Alfred's grandson, and the first of his house to use the title 'King of England'.

Edgar the Peaceful, here shown with crown, orb, and sceptre, in the full regalia as 'Lord of Britain'.

The only existing portraits of the Wessex kings are to be seen on the coinage of their time. These Saxon silver pennies often show the profile of the king on one side, the obverse, and king's name, often with that of the moneyer on the other, the reverse.

Although the king's head shows different features in different reigns, there appears to be a traditional stylized pattern which the authorities believe to be copied from, or to derive from the Roman coinage. This may be why none of the Wessex kings are shown to have beards on the coinage of their own time.

The profiles of Edgar, and his two sons do not have beards, but the later, Danish kings, and Edgar's grandson Edward the Confessor, all wear beards. It remains an open question whether any of the earlier kings wore facial hair, but these stained glass kings in Wells are probably 'Victorian' so how could they not have beards?

Only those with very good eyesight will be able to see in the south transept at Wells, hidden away in the tracery at the very top of the most westerly of the south facing windows, preserved in the medieval glass there, archbishop Dunstan tweaking the devil's nose with a pair of tongs.

Ceramic:

A china medallion or plaque, painted, possibly for the coronation of Queen Victoria, attempted to show Edgar's coronation as the artist thought the eye witness described it. The plaque which was in the royal collection is now lost or broken. It does not appear in any catalogue, but the medallion may still be seen as an illustration in Meehan's book *Historic Houses in Bath and District* published in 1904.

Heraldry:

The arms attributed to King Edgar and his two sons may be seen in Bath Abbey. The shield is high up on the north east wall where springs the fan vaulting of the old stone roof of the choir, and very near to the present high altar.

The shield shows:

Azure, a cross flory, between four doves or

In non-heraldic terms, this reads:

On a blue background, a gold cross with floriated arms, between four golden doves.

The Old English Chronicles

The *Anglo-Saxon Chronicle*

There are in existence at least six versions, recensions, or revisions of the *Anglo-Saxon Chronicle*. These annals date back to the earliest settlement of the Anglo-Saxons in this country, and to events concerning the spread of Christianity even before this time. The chronicler wrote down the year and any event of importance that had occurred during that year. The recensions of the *Chronicle* still in existence were probably written between the ninth and eleventh centuries. Earlier annals were used, and events were often recorded many years after they had occurred. Chroniclers in monasteries in different parts of the country compiled or copied the annals over the three centuries. There were different hands, variations in expression, and chronology, in the six recensions over the years. Professor Whitelock's edition of the most recent comparative selection from these annals has been used here.

Ethelweard's Chronicle

These annals were written by a layman of the late tenth century, a kinsman and friend of King Edgar. Ethelweard wrote very soon after Edgar's death, and according to Stenton his chronicle is based on the text of an Anglo-Saxon Chronicle different from all other surviving texts, which he translated into very indifferent Latin for the benefit of a German kinswoman who was like himself, a descendant of the royal house of Wessex.

The Chronicle of Florence of Worcester

These annals, also based on the *Anglo-Saxon Chronicle* and other sources, are thought to have been written by a monk of Worcester at the beginning of the twelfth century. There is a translation by J. Stevenson in: *The Church Historians of England*, Vol. 2, London, 1853. Florence is also believed to have had access to earlier documents now lost.

Charters

Anglo-Saxon Charters referred to in the text are usually concerned with grants of land.

The Bath Charters are all to be found in Vol. VII, Somerset Record Society publications.

Early Charters of the West Midlands and *Early Charters of Wessex* by H. P. R. Finberg, Leicester University Press, 1961, 1964. The charters in these volumes are so arranged that the take over of Bath from Mercia into Wessex in Alfred's time is clearly shown.

The Abingdon Charters (*Chronicles of the Monastery of Abingdon*) are among those which show the disappearance of ealdorman Ethelwold's name as a testator to charters in the year 962, the year of his death. The name of his brother Ethelwine appears in its place as one of Edgar's senior ealdormen, thus disproving the fantastic legend that Edgar killed his close friend and foster brother Ethelwold, so that he would be able to marry his widow.

Bede's *History of the English Church and People* has been translated into English by Leo Sherley-Price for the Penquin Classics series. Bede is the greatest of the old English writers. His *History* written about the year 731 is the most remarkable work not only of the Anglo-Saxon period but for many centuries after.

BIBLIOGRAPHY
(Works referred to in the text only)

Abbreviation

A.S.C.   The *Anglo-Saxon Chronicle*. Ed. D. Whitelock   1965
E.H.D.   *English Historical Documents*, Vol. I. Ed. D.
                  Whitelock   1955
Malmesbury,
  William   *Chronicles of the Kings of England*. Ed. J. A. Giles   1848
Ethelweard(in)   *Six Old English Chronicles*. Ed. J. A. Giles   1848
Ethelweard's   *Chronicle*. Published Nelson. Ed. A. Campbell   1962
Abingdon   *Chronicles of the Monastery of Abingdon*. Rolls Series.
                  Ed. J. Stevenson   1858
Asser   Asser's *Life of Alfred* Ed. J. A. Giles   1848
                                             Ed. W. H. Stevenson   1904
Robertson   *Historical Essays*. E. W. Robertson, Edinburgh   1872
Ramsey   Chronicle of Ramsey Abbey. Rolls Series   1886
Stubbs   *Memorials of St. Dunstan*. Rolls Series. Ed. W.
                  Stubbs   1874
Raine   *Historians of the Church of York*, Vol. I. Rolls Series.
                  Ed. J. Raine (*Vita Oswaldi*)   1879
Davis   *Notes on the Hot Mineral Baths of Bath*. C. E. Davis,
                  Bath   1885
S.R.S.   *Two Cartularies of St. Peter's, Bath*. Somerset Record
                  Society, Vol. VII
A.D.   *Ancient Deeds of Bath*. Ed. Rev. J. Shickle   1921
Wells MSS.   *A Calendar of Mss. of the Dean and Chapter of Wells*,
                  Vol. I. H.M. Stationery Office   1907
Leland   *Itinerary in England* (1535–1543). Ed. L. Toulmin-
                  Smith, London   1907
Whitelock (3)   *The Beginnings of English Society*. D. Whitelock.
                  Pelican   1952
Stenton   *Anglo-Saxon England*. Sir Frank Stenton. O.U.P.   1943
Hodgkin   *A History of the Anglo-Saxons*. R. H. Hodgkin.
                  O.U.P.   1935
Levison   *England and the Continent in the Eighth Century*.
                  W. Levison, London   1946
Robinson   *The Times of St. Dunstan*. J. Armitage Robinson.
                  O.U.P.   1923
Schramm   *History of the English Coronation*. P. E. Schramm.
                  O.U.P.   1937
P.S.A.S.   *Proceedings of the Somerset Archaeological Society*   1964
R. and S.   *The Governance of Medieval England*. Richardson &
                  Sayles, Edinburgh   1963

REFERENCES

		page
1.	Stubbs (quoting Robertson)	8
2.	Stenton, p. 363	9
3.	E.H.D., Vol. I, p. 944	15
4.	Raine, *Vita Oswaldi*	17
5.	Malmesbury, p. 159	18
6.	Asser, A.D. 877	18
7.	Stenton, p. 343	19
8.	E.H.D., Vol. I, p. 395	19
9.	Stenton, p. 363	20
10.	E.H.D., Vol. I, p. 258	21
11.	Whitelock (3), p. 152	23
12.	Robertson, p. 175	25
13.	Stubbs, note 3, p. C.	26
14.	Stenton, p. 443	28
15.	Robinson, p. 89	29
16.	Schramm, pp. 23–24	37
17.	Raine, pp. 436–8	38
18.	Robertson, p. 206	38
19.	Schramm, pp. 19–20	40
20.	Stenton, p. 365	41
21.	Levison, p. 31	41
22.	S.R.S., Vol. VII, 1, 39	43
23.	Wells MSS., Vol. 1, p. 473	44
24.	P.S.A.S., 1964	45
25.	Hodgkin, p. 390	45
26.	V.C.H. Dorset, Vol. 2, p. 73	49
27.	Stenton, p. 361	52
28.	Raine, p. 428	52
29.	Malmesbury, p. 147	53
30.	Leland, p. 143	53